Teaching with
Look, Listen, and Speak

What Is *Look, Listen, and Speak*?

Evan-Moor's *Look, Listen, and Speak* is a theme-based series designed to build vocabulary and language patterns for young English learners and other students who can benefit from language enrichment.

Who Should Use *Look, Listen, and Speak*?

The multiple resources in *Look, Listen, and Speak* may be used in a variety of instructional settings. Use them for:

- teacher-directed group lessons in class or during pull-out instruction,
- independent or partner work at a computer in class or in a computer lab,
- peer or cross-grade tutoring activities, and
- classroom learning center activities.

Look, Listen, and Speak can help you meet your students' needs, whether you have one or two English learners or a larger group.

What Makes *Look, Listen, and Speak* So Flexible?

- The multiple components in *Look, Listen, and Speak* (see pages 2 and 3) provide various options for introducing and practicing new material. Vocabulary and language patterns may be introduced during teacher-directed lessons, or by using the interactive computer program.

- Students can progress at their own individual pace when they use the interactive computer activities. Risk-free computer learning also encourages even the most self-conscious learners to try out new language.

- Sample scripts model language appropriate for students at different stages of language development, helping you to expand students' language production. Para-professionals, volunteers, and peer or cross-grade tutors can guide English learners through simple lessons and follow-up activities.

What About Reading in *Look, Listen, and Speak*?

The goal of *Look, Listen, and Speak* is to build vocabulary and English fluency for learners. Although there is no direct instruction in reading per se, students will have many opportunities to relate spoken language to text.

Vocabulary items are labeled on the Print Poster. On the E-poster, these labels appear on the screen as the audio pronounces each word. Similarly, words in the text of the Chants and Storybook are individually highlighted as they are spoken aloud on the computer. As students become familiar with the memorable language of chants and rhymes, they may be able to "read" this text on the computer or on the reproducible pages.

Learning Resources in
Look, Listen, and Speak

Print Poster

At the Park includes a Print Poster featuring a detailed scene that allows you to introduce new vocabulary in a meaningful context. The Print Poster also includes labels for key thematic vocabulary. (See page 6 for guidance on using the Print Poster to introduce vocabulary.)

Electronic Posters (E-posters)

At the Park includes one main E-poster (presenting the same image as on the Print Poster) and one additional E-poster. Students scroll over images in the scene to hear the word spoken aloud and used in a sentence. A label for each word also appears, and animations help enhance meaning for some words. (See page 8 for guidance on using the E-posters to introduce vocabulary.)

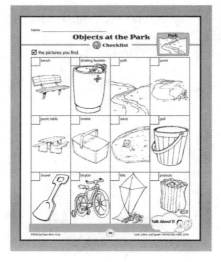

Reproducibles

Reproducible pages are used for a variety of activities. They include:

- Checklists to track new vocabulary items presented on the Print Poster and the E-posters,
- follow-up activities to reinforce new vocabulary after it is introduced and templates for creating individual student wordbooks,
- interactive games to spark meaningful language, and
- text of rhymes, chants, and stories to help build language fluency.

Look, Listen, and Speak—At the Park • EMC 2740

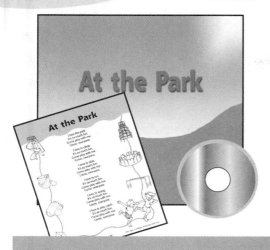

Chants

At the Park includes several theme-related rhymes, chants, or songs. Memorable, rhyming language and simple melodies help students internalize thematic vocabulary and new language patterns, building fluency in a fun, low-stress manner. When viewed on the computer, text is highlighted as students hear each word. Reproducible versions of each Chant may be used to create student booklets, to send home with students, or for group performances in class.

Storybook

Simple, rhyming, patterned, or predictable stories provide another context for students to use vocabulary and language patterns presented in the unit. Students have two options for experiencing the simple, theme-related eight-page story:

- The electronic Storybook on the CD-ROM highlights each word in the simple text as it is pronounced.

- The reproducible Storybook may be used to create individual booklets for students to take home or use in class for individual, partner, or group reading.

Electronic Games (E-games)

Electronic Games provide a fun way to reinforce new vocabulary and language patterns. Students listen and follow directions to move pieces on game boards and participate in other motivating activities such as moving through mazes and assembling puzzle pieces. Simple commands redirect students to try again as needed, and positive reinforcement is provided for successful completion of game tasks.

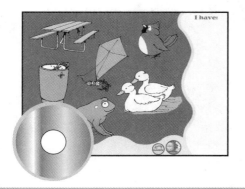

Games with Picture Cards

At the Park includes a set of 48 Picture Cards representing vocabulary from the theme. Suggestions are included for using the Picture Cards to reinforce vocabulary development. Directions for games using the Picture Cards are also included. As partners or small groups use the Picture Cards to play, they have lots of opportunities to use language for purposeful communication.

Look, Listen, and Speak—At the Park • EMC 2740

About the
CD-ROM

Installing the Program

1 Put the CD in your CD-ROM drive.

The installation program will start automatically. If it doesn't, access the CD-ROM drive on your computer and double-click on the icon labeled *Install*.

Follow the instructions to install *Look, Listen, and Speak*.

The installation application will place a shortcut to *Look, Listen, and Speak* on your desktop.

2 To launch *Look, Listen, and Speak*, double-click on the shortcut on your desktop.

You will arrive at the main menu.

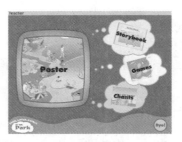

Main Menu Features

The main menu displays the six features of the *Look, Listen, and Speak* program.

Teacher
- View E-book
- Quit

E-poster

Storybook

Games

Chants

Bye!
closes the program

The E-book

The complete book is presented in printable electronic format. Access the E-book through the "Teacher" menu. You must have Adobe® Acrobat® Reader® installed on your computer to view the E-book. You have the option of installing Adobe® Acrobat® Reader® when you install the *Look, Listen, and Speak* program.

Building Vocabulary

Using the Posters

Students acquire vocabulary most successfully when the words they are learning all relate to a central concept. In *Look, Listen, and Speak,* thematic Print and Electronic Posters provide rich visual context to enhance comprehension of new vocabulary. The Posters, therefore, are the primary resource for introducing vocabulary.

Directed Lesson

See "Using the Print Poster" below if you plan to conduct a directed lesson with the Print Poster to present new vocabulary for a topic.

Independent Practice

If you plan to have students work independently at the computer to acquire new vocabulary for a topic, see "Using the Electronic Poster" on page 8.

Be sure that new vocabulary for each topic has been introduced through a directed lesson or a lesson at the computer before students complete follow-up activities or create Wordbook pages for that topic.

Students should be encouraged to experience the Chants and the Storybook on the CD-ROM as often as they wish. Conduct the directed lessons for these activities after you have introduced the related vocabulary.

Using the Print Poster

The vocabulary for this unit has been grouped by topics. Depending on your students' English proficiency, you may wish to present vocabulary for more than one topic during a directed lesson. To use the Poster to introduce vocabulary:

- choose the topic or topics you will present from the list on page 5,

- reproduce a copy of the appropriate topic Checklist to guide you in presenting vocabulary,

- review the sample script on page 7, noting the strategies for introducing vocabulary and expanding language, and

- for other topics, use the strategies presented in the sample script as a model, adapting the language to fit the vocabulary presented for each topic.

After students have completed the activities in this unit, you may also use the Poster and Checklists to conduct a verbal assessment of students' acquisition of new vocabulary from the unit.

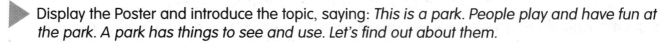

Sample Script

▶ Display the Poster and introduce the topic, saying: *This is a park. People play and have fun at the park. A park has things to see and use. Let's find out about them.*

▶ Following the order of the items on the topic Checklist, point to and name each place or item, using simple language such as: *This is a bench. Now you say it…Yes, this is a bench. People sit on a bench. This is a drinking fountain. You say it now…Good. You can get a drink of water at a drinking fountain. The bench and the drinking fountain are in the park.* Use similar language to introduce *path, pond, picnic table,* and *basket.*

You can play at the park. (Point to the sand.) This is sand. You say it now…Good! You can play in the sand. Repeat, please…(Point to the shovel.) This is a shovel. Repeat, please… Good! You can dig in the sand with the shovel. You can put the sand in the pail. Use similar language as well as pantomime and gestures to introduce *bicycle* and *kite.*

Point to the peanut in the man's hand. *This is a peanut. Now you say it…Yes, this is a peanut. People eat peanuts. Animals eat peanuts, too. The man is giving peanuts to the squirrel to eat.*

Strategies for Expanding and Practicing Language

Once you introduce all items on the Checklist, choose the strategies appropriate for your students' language level to review new vocabulary by posing questions and eliciting language as modeled below.

Beginning Students	Encourage students to respond nonverbally by pointing out items on the Poster in response to prompts such as: *Show me the path. Point to the sand. Where is the drinking fountain?*, etc. Then model verbal responses for students to repeat: *You're right. This is the drinking fountain. Now you say it: This is the drinking fountain.*
Intermediate Students	Elicit yes/no responses with prompts such as: *Is this the path?* Use questions that model language for students by embedding answer choices: *Is this the pail or the shovel?* Encourage students to answer in complete sentences: *Good. Now say the whole thing: This is the shovel.*
Advanced Students	Use questions that encourage students to elaborate, such as: *Why is there a bench and a drinking fountain in the park? What can you do with the sand at the park?*

As students gain greater proficiency, be sure to use increasingly challenging prompts as you conduct directed lessons, thereby encouraging the production of more language.

Look, Listen, and Speak—At the Park • EMC 2740

Using the Electronic Poster (E-poster)

Components of an E-poster Lesson

Poster on the CD-ROM

When you click on the E-poster on the main menu, you will see this screen showing "The Park." This is the main E-poster for *At the Park*.

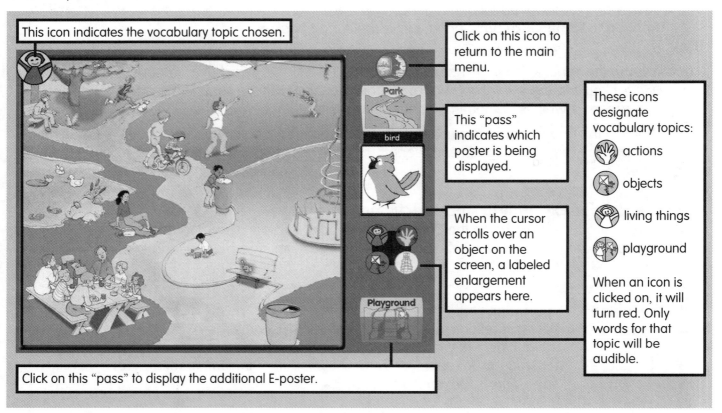

This icon indicates the vocabulary topic chosen.

Click on this icon to return to the main menu.

This "pass" indicates which poster is being displayed.

When the cursor scrolls over an object on the screen, a labeled enlargement appears here.

These icons designate vocabulary topics:

actions

objects

living things

playground

When an icon is clicked on, it will turn red. Only words for that topic will be audible.

Click on this "pass" to display the additional E-poster.

Reproducible Activities

Checklists—In the "Building Vocabulary" section, pages 10–37, you will find Checklists focusing on the various vocabulary topics. The Checklists let students know which items on the screen to scroll over.

This icon shows the vocabulary topic.

This icon shows the E-poster to choose.

Follow-up Activities to Reinforce Vocabulary
The "Talk About It" feature prompts students to interact orally about the content on the page. This is a key element in practicing new language, and it provides an opportunity for informal assessment of language acquisition.

E-poster Lesson Steps

Preparation

Choose the topic or topics you wish to present from the list on page 6.

Reproduce a copy of the topic Checklist(s) for each student.
Reproduce the follow-up activities if desired.

Learning New Vocabulary

You may wish to model one or two lessons until students are familiar with the steps.

1 On the main menu screen, click on the E-poster.

2 Choose the E-poster and topic shown on the Checklist. (See page 8.)

3 Instruct students to find an item from the Checklist on the screen and begin to scroll over it.

- When the cursor is directly over the item, students will hear its name.
- When students click on the item, they hear a complete sentence, including the topic word.
- A labeled, closeup view of the item appears in the box on the right, and animation shows details for some objects.

sand

4 Students listen to each item as many times as they wish, repeating what they hear when they are ready.

5 Students check off that item on their Checklist.

6 When all of the items on the Checklist have been practiced, students may review them again, move on to another topic, or end their session.

7 After students complete a lesson with the E-poster, have them name each of the items on the Checklist for you, another adult, or another student.

8 If you wish, students may complete the follow-up activity at this time.

Increasing Interaction

Students may also work with partners or in small groups to learn and practice vocabulary using the E-poster. For partner work, pair a student with greater English proficiency with a beginning-level student. As noted above, students use the Checklist to guide them through the clickable elements on the E-poster. Then the more proficient student may use the Checklist to direct his or her partner in practicing and reviewing the new vocabulary: *Find the pond. Click on the fountain,* etc. The more proficient student may also encourage a partner to listen to and repeat language to improve pronunciation.

Small groups may follow a similar procedure, working with an English-proficient leader (a teacher or another adult, or a peer or cross-grade tutor).

Name _____

Objects at the Park
Checklist

☑ the pictures you find.

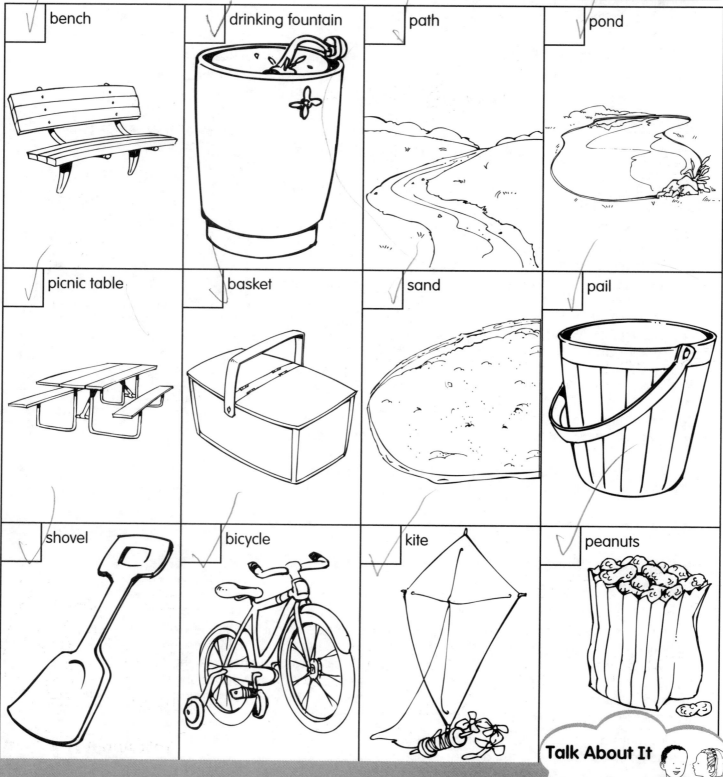

bench	drinking fountain	path	pond
picnic table	basket	sand	pail
shovel	bicycle	kite	peanuts

Talk About It

Note: The student colors and cuts out the pictures, and then pastes them in the correct circles.

Name _____

Who Goes Here?

Park

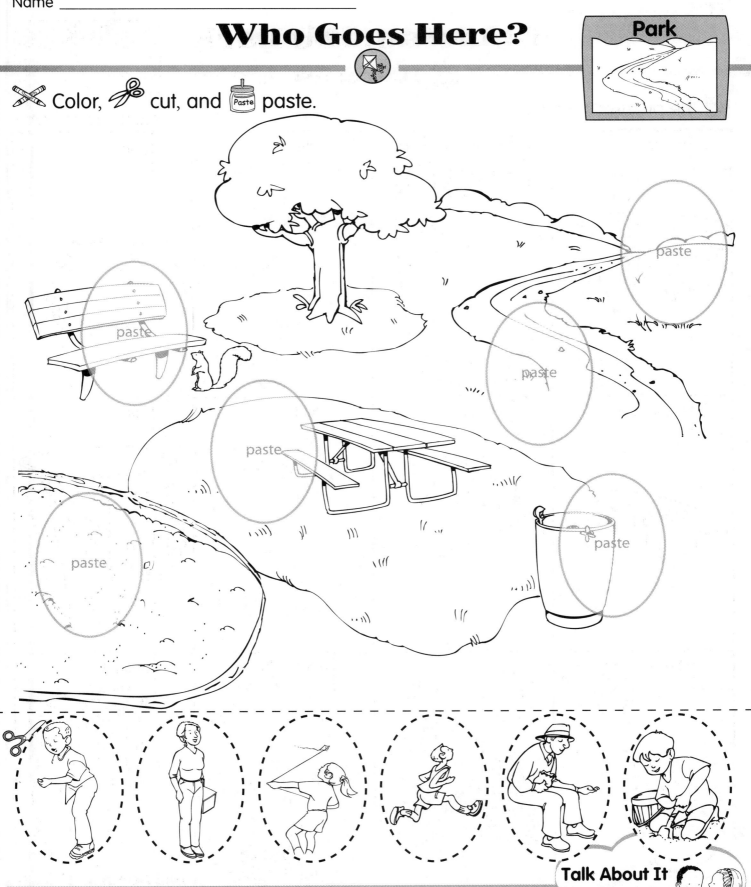

✎ Color, ✂ cut, and [Paste] paste.

Look, Listen, and Speak—At the Park • EMC 2740

Name _____

Living Things

 **Checklist**

☑ the pictures you find.

boy	girl	man	woman
dog	bird	squirrel	ducks
fish	frog	grass	tree

Talk About It

Note: Review the difference between something that is alive and not alive, using examples from the Poster. Then have students circle *is* or *is not* to tell if the item shown is living. Have students say their responses aloud to someone.

Name _____

Is It Alive?

Park

Circle the answer.

A duck ____ alive.	A tree ____ alive.	A bench ____ alive.	A girl ____ alive.
is is not	**is is not**	**is is not**	**is is not**

A bird ____ alive.	A kite ____ alive.	A table ____ alive.	A fish ____ alive.
is is not	**is is not**	**is is not**	**is is not**

A shovel ____ alive.	A boy ____ alive.	A man ____ alive.	Sand ____ alive.
is is not	**is is not**	**is is not**	**is is not**

Talk About It

Look, Listen, and Speak—At the Park • EMC 2740

Name _____

Living Things

 Cut out the pictures. Paste them in the correct boxes.

Animals

paste	paste
paste	paste
paste	paste

People

paste	paste
paste	paste

Plants

paste	paste

bird	boy	dog	girl	grass	squirrel
man	ducks	frog	woman	tree	fish

Talk About It

Look, Listen, and Speak—At the Park • EMC 2740

Do You Have It?
A Partner Activity

Name _____

Do You Have It? **A**

Look, Listen, and Speak—At the Park • EMC 2740

Name _____

Do You Have It? **B**

Look, Listen, and Speak—At the Park • EMC 2740

Name _____

Actions
✋ Checklist

☑ the pictures you find.

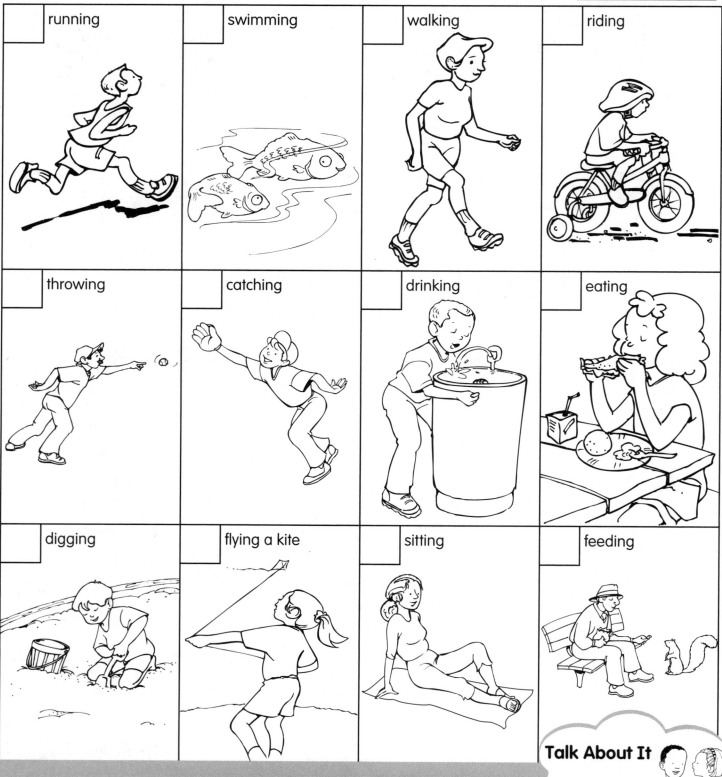

☐ running	☐ swimming	☐ walking	☐ riding
☐ throwing	☐ catching	☐ drinking	☐ eating
☐ digging	☐ flying a kite	☐ sitting	☐ feeding

Talk About It

Name _____

What Am I Doing?

Park

Write the missing word.

running

flying

riding

throwing

eating

drinking

He is _____ a ball. He is _____ water. She is _____ a kite.

They are _____. She is _____. He is _____.

Talk About It

Note: Use these pictures and the sentences on page 19 to review the sequence of events in the family's picnic at the park. Students then cut out the pictures on this page and paste them in order in the boxes on page 19. Students may use their own words to describe the pictures; they may be prompted to provide descriptions (*What did they do next?*); or they may echo each sentence after a partner reads it aloud.

A Picnic at the Park

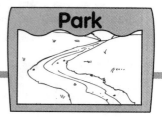

Part 1

 Color.  Cut.  Paste in order.

 Talk About It

Look, Listen, and Speak—At the Park • EMC 2740

A Picnic at the Park

Part 2

The family went to the park for a picnic.

They sat down at a picnic table.

Mom took food out of the picnic basket.

The family ate a picnic lunch.

They cleaned up the garbage.

The family went home.

Talk About It

Name _____

Yes or No?

Park

Circle **yes** or **no** to answer the questions.

Do you like to throw a ball?

yes   no

Do you like to fly a kite?

yes   no

Do you like to dig in the sand?

yes   no

Do you like to run?

yes   no

Do you like to ride a bike?

yes   no

Do you like to feed the squirrels?

yes   no

Talk About It

Look, Listen, and Speak—At the Park • EMC 2740

Name _____

Playground Equipment

 Checklist

Playground

☑ the pictures you find.

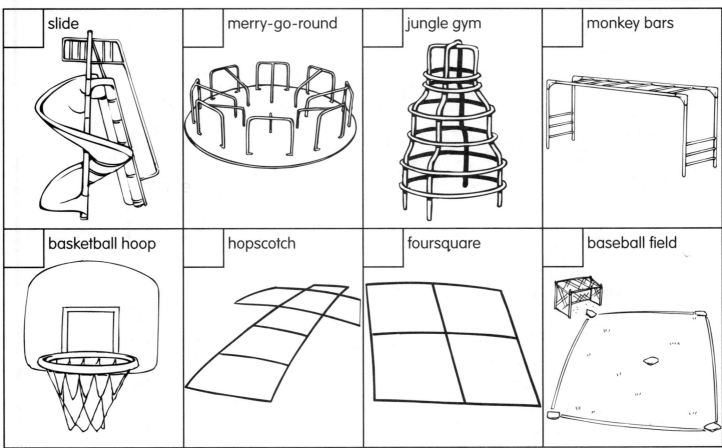

| slide | merry-go-round | jungle gym | monkey bars |
| basketball hoop | hopscotch | foursquare | baseball field |

☑ the equipment you have used.

☐ slide ☐ basketball hoop

☐ merry-go-round ☐ hopscotch

☐ jungle gym ☐ foursquare

☐ monkey bars ☐ baseball

Talk About It

Look, Listen, and Speak—At the Park • EMC 2740

Name _____

Where Am I?

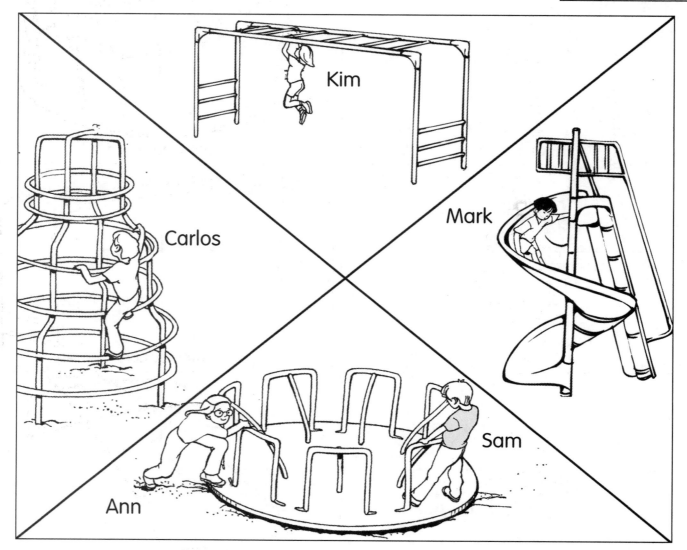

Kim

Carlos

Mark

Sam

Ann

_____ is on the jungle gym.

_____ and _____ are on the merry-go-round.

_____ is on the monkey bars.

_____ is on the slide.

Talk About It

Look, Listen, and Speak—At the Park • EMC 2740

Concentration Cards

slide

merry-go-round

jungle gym

monkey bars

basketball hoop

hopscotch

foursquare

baseball field

Look, Listen, and Speak—At the Park • EMC 2740

Name _____

Playground Actions

 **Checklist**

☑ the pictures you find.

| waiting | pushing | climbing | swinging |
| throwing | running | hopping | bouncing |

✎ Draw yourself playing on the playground.

Talk About It

Playtime

1. ✂ Cut out the ☐ and ☐.

2. Fold and cut the viewer.

3. Put the strip in the viewer.

4. Pull the strip. Read the words.

✂ -

fold ——— cut ——— cut ——— fold

©2003 by Evan-Moor Corp.

Look, Listen, and Speak—At the Park • EMC 2740

pull

What they did at the park:

She climbed.

She hopped.

She threw.

He ran.

He bounced a ball.

Name _____

What Are They Going to Do?

Look at the picture. What will the children do?

bounce

climb

hop

She will _____ on the hopscotch.

He will _____ the ball.

He will _____ on the jungle gym.

Draw what you like to do at the playground.

I like to _____ at the playground.

Talk About It

Note: Using the Print Poster as a guide, the student finds the items shown below and colors them the same colors as on the Poster. The student writes the correct color word on the line, finds something else on the Poster that is the same color, draws it on the right-hand side of the page, and writes its name on the line.

Name _____

Color Hunt

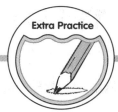

Extra Practice

red	yellow	blue	green
purple	brown	orange	black

Look at the poster. Find the picture.

Color it.	Draw it.
The picnic table is _____.	The _____ is, too.
The garbage can is _____.	The _____ is, too.
The frog is _____.	The _____ is, too.

Talk About It

Look, Listen, and Speak—At the Park • EMC 2740

Name _____

What Is Missing?

Draw what is missing.

Talk About It

Note: Students draw themselves doing the activities they like to do at the park, complete each sentence, and practice the patterned language with a partner.

Name _____

What Do You Like?

Extra Practice

Draw what you like to do at the park. Finish each sentence.

They like to play catch.	I like _____.
She likes to ride a bike.	I like _____.
He likes to dig in the sand.	I like _____.
They like to eat at the park.	I like _____.
He likes to run in the park.	I like _____.

Talk About It

Look, Listen, and Speak—At the Park • EMC 2740

Note: First, students refer to the poster to find items that are bigger and smaller than the squirrel, boy, and picnic basket, and then draw them in the appropriate boxes. Second, students write the appropriate words to describe the relative sizes of the frog and dog.

Name _____

Bigger and Smaller

✏ Draw a picture in each box. Write the names on the line.

bigger　　　　　　　　　　　　　　　　　　　　　**smaller**

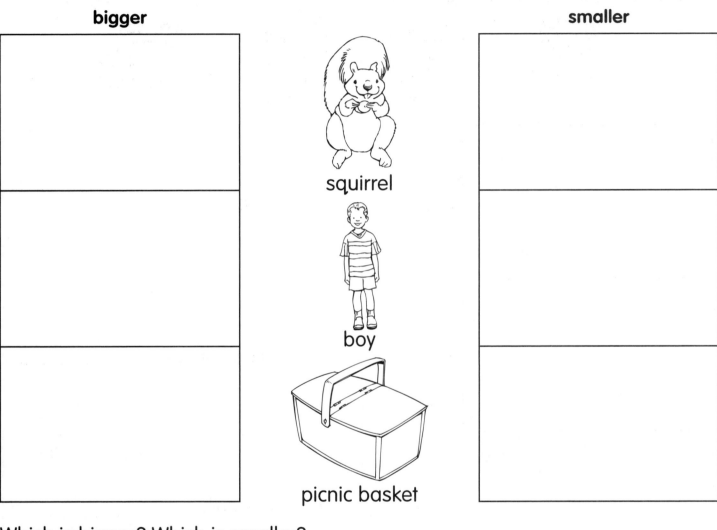

squirrel

boy

picnic basket

Which is bigger? Which is smaller?

frog 　　　dog

The _____ is bigger than the _____.

The _____ is smaller than the _____.

Talk About It

Note: Explain how the little pictures below show position. Students use the Print Poster to find something that is in each position to complete the sentences, and then draw a picture to show the answer.

Name _____

Where Is It?

Look at the poster. Find something in each place.

Draw it in the box. Write it on the lines.

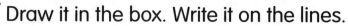

on   under   next to   in

The _____ is **in** the _____.

The _____ is **under** the _____.

The _____ is **on** the _____.

The _____ is **next to** the _____.

Talk About It

Look, Listen, and Speak—At the Park • EMC 2740

My Wordbook

Students create a Wordbook containing the vocabulary learned from the Posters. Add a page to the book after each area of the Poster has been covered.

Materials

- paste
- scissors
- pencil
- 12″ x 16″ (30.5 x 41 cm) colored construction paper

Steps to Follow

1. Make a cover for the Wordbook by folding the construction paper in half and pasting the cover picture on the front. Store pages of the Wordbook in this folder. When all Wordbook pages have been completed, staple them inside the folder.

2. For each page of the Wordbook, students color and cut out the pictures of the words studied. They then paste one picture in each box on the Wordbook template. If they need help in matching an item with its name, students may revisit the E-posters.

3. Students copy the name of the picture on the corresponding writing line.

4. As each page is completed, have students work with a partner to name the items on the page or use them in a sentence before adding the page to their Wordbook. Encourage students to refer to their Wordbook as needed for vocabulary support.

My Wordbook

name

EMC 2740

©2003 by Evan-Moor Corp.

My Wordbook

paste

bench

paste

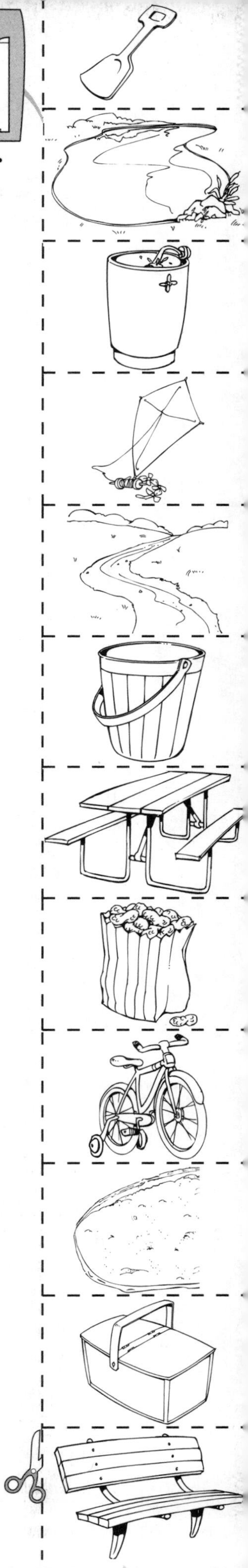

bicycle

paste

drinking fountain

paste

kite

paste

pail

paste

path

paste

peanuts

paste

picnic basket

paste

picnic table

paste

pond

paste

sand

paste

shovel

My Wordbook

Living Things

paste	paste
bird _____	boy _____
paste	paste
dog _____	ducks _____
paste	paste
fish _____	frog _____
paste	paste
girl _____	grass _____
paste	paste
man _____	squirrel _____
paste	paste
tree _____	woman _____

My Wordbook

Actions

paste	paste
catching	digging
paste	paste
drinking	eating
paste	paste
feeding	flying a kite
paste	paste
riding	running
paste	paste
sitting	swimming
paste	paste
throwing	walking

My Wordbook

paste	paste
baseball field _____	basketball hoop _____
paste	paste
foursquare _____	hopscotch _____
paste	paste
jungle gym _____	merry-go-round _____
paste	paste
monkey bars _____	slide _____

My Wordbook

paste	paste
bouncing	climbing

paste	paste
hopping	pushing

paste	paste
running	swinging

paste	paste
throwing	waiting

Building Fluency

Stages and Strategies in Building Fluency

	Students	Their Teachers
Beginning	• need a lot of practice with the sounds and patterns of English • respond nonverbally with gestures or drawings • repeat words and phrases • rely on picture clues to facilitate understanding • show some comprehension of familiar expressions	• use visuals, real objects, gestures, and pantomime to support active listening • use chants, songs, and shared reading to model language • pair beginners with more advanced students for practice • have students label objects, manipulate pictures, and create original artwork
Intermediate	• become more confident in using English • show greater comprehension of spoken language • use familiar expressions in speech • identify people, places, and things • speak in simple, complete sentences	• continue to pair students with more advanced learners • continue providing opportunities for listening comprehension • use questions to elicit language (Who? What? Where?, etc.) • use techniques for enriching language expression (expanding, restating, etc.) • provide opportunities for conversations and discussions
Advanced	• speak in longer phrases and sentences • use more extensive vocabulary • participate in discussions • are able to compare, describe, and retell in English • do some reading in English • do some writing in English	• provide varied opportunities for students to express themselves orally or in print • use techniques for enriching language expression (expanding, restating, etc.) • provide materials to promote conceptual development (textbooks, trade books, etc.)

Using the Chants

Before students can produce new language structures and patterns, they must hear them enough to internalize them. The rhythmic and rhyming language of chants, rhymes, and songs make them a memorable language form. As students echo, repeat, and recite chants, they begin to internalize new language patterns and structures, and to use new vocabulary in meaningful contexts. Reciting chants as part of a group or during interaction at the computer also helps reduce the stress of trying out new language.

In addition, the CD-ROM displays the text of the Chants and highlights each word as it is pronounced, helping foster word recognition and strengthening sound-symbol associations.

Encourage students to listen to the Chants on the *Look, Listen, and Speak* CD-ROM as often as they like to help them internalize new language. Conduct group activities with the Chants as soon as you have introduced the vocabulary in each Chant with a Poster lesson.

Use any of these options to provide students with a variety of experiences:

- Conduct directed group lessons with the Chants (see pages 40, 42, 44), displaying text on the CD-ROM through a digital projector, or using the reproducible page to create an overhead transparency.

- Have individuals, partners, or small groups play the Chants on the CD-ROM.

- Make individual copies of the reproducible page for students to take home or collect in a chant folder.

Using the Storybook

The Storybook provides another source of memorable language patterns and structures. Written in simple, patterned, predictable, or rhyming language, the Storybook also offers additional experience with theme-related content and vocabulary. The CD-ROM version highlights each word in the text as it is pronounced, helping build word recognition and developing sound-symbol relationships for emerging readers of English.

These options will provide students with a variety of experiences with the Storybook:

- After introducing the vocabulary in the Storybook with a Poster lesson, use the reproducible Storybook (pages 47–50) to conduct the directed lesson on page 46.

- After students are familiar with the story, encourage them to experience the E-storybook on the CD-ROM as often as they wish. Model how to "turn the pages," and turn on the audio to hear the text as it is highlighted.

- Have students use the reproducible Storybook for rereading and follow-up activities as outlined on pages 51 and 52.

What Will You Do?
A Chant

Materials

- *What Will You Do?* displayed on a computer monitor, digital projector, or overhead projector
- Picture Cards 28–43

Review Vocabulary

Use the Picture Cards to review vocabulary. As you hold up each card, invite a volunteer to name the action. Have the group echo with a word or a complete sentence: *Digging. He is digging.* Repeat with each picture card. If students are unable to respond correctly, provide the answer and ask students to echo your response. Extend the activity by asking for a volunteer to pantomime the action. Explain to students that they will learn a chant about things you can do at the park.

Model the Chant

Present *What Will You Do?* line by line, pointing to the text in the chant. Repeat this procedure once or twice before inviting students to join you in reciting the chant all together. Select a student to ask the question each time. The rest of the group responds with the answer. This chant is set up in a chain format: Speaker 1 asks. Speaker 2 answers. Speaker 2 asks. Speaker 3 answers, etc. When students are comfortable with the chant, assign parts to students and have them say the complete rhyme.

Repeat Performances

Use these ideas when you revisit the chant:

- Listen and Recite
  Encourage individuals or partners to chime in on the *What Will You Do?* chant as it is played on the CD-ROM.

- Innovations
  Write the chant form on a chart or the chalkboard, leaving out the action.

  > *At the park,*
  > *What will _____ do?*
  > *I'll _____.*
  > *How about you?*

  Work with students to fill in the missing words to write new verses for the Chant. Have students copy and illustrate one of the new verses. These may be placed in a construction paper cover to create a class book.

- Send It Home
  Reproduce page 41 for students to take home and share with their families.

What Will You Do?

At the park, what will you do?

I'll dig in the sand.
How about you?

At the park, what will you do?

I'll go down the slide.
How about you?

At the park, what will you do?

I'll feed the ducks.
How about you?

At the park, what will you do?

I'll have a picnic.
How about you?

At the park, what will you do?

I'll play catch with a ball.
How about you?

At the park, what will you do?

I'll run with my dog.
How about you?

Look, Listen, and Speak—At the Park • EMC 2740

At the Park
A Chant

Materials

- *At the Park* displayed on a computer monitor, digital projector, or overhead projector
- Picture Cards 28–43

Review Vocabulary

Use the Picture Cards to review action vocabulary. As you hold up each card, invite a volunteer to name the action. Have the group echo with a word or a complete sentence. *Hopping: She is hopping.* Ask for a volunteer to pantomime the action.

Model the Chant

Establish a beat with hand clapping or finger snapping. Then use a call-and-response format to present *At the Park* line by line, pointing to the text in the chant. Repeat this procedure once or twice before inviting students to join you in reciting the chant all together. Then divide the students into two groups. One group recites the first two lines of each stanza, and the other group recites the remaining lines.

Repeat Performances

Use these ideas when you revisit the chant:

- <u>Listen and Recite</u>
  Encourage individuals or partners to chime in on the *At the Park* chant as it is played on the CD-ROM.

- <u>Innovations</u>
  Discuss other things you might do at the park. Then ask each child in the group to choose the one they like best and substitute it as they recite the verse.

  > *I love to _____.*
  > *It's so much fun.*
  > *Come play with me.*
  > *Come, everyone.*

  Extend the activity by asking students to illustrate themselves doing the action. More able students may also copy the verse, writing in the new action.

- <u>Send It Home</u>
  Reproduce page 43 for students to take home and share with their families.

At the Park

I love the park.
It's so much fun.
Come play with me.
Come, everyone.

I love to climb.
It's so much fun.
Come play with me.
Come, everyone.

I love to slide.
It's so much fun.
Come play with me.
Come, everyone.

I love to run.
It's so much fun.
Come play with me.
Come, everyone.

I love to swing.
It's so much fun.
Come play with me.
Come, everyone.

I love to play catch.
It's so much fun.
Come play with me.
Come, everyone.

Look, Listen, and Speak—At the Park • EMC 2740

One Sunny Day
A Song

Materials

- *One Sunny Day* displayed on a computer monitor, digital projector, or overhead projector

Review Vocabulary

Ask, *What do you do when you go to the park?* List these actions on the chalkboard. When the list is complete, read each word aloud one at a time and select a student to act it out. Describe what the student did using a complete sentence: *He jumped. She ran.*

Model the Song

Say, *This song is about what some children did when they went to the park on a sunny day.* Then listen to the song (sung to the tune of "The Mulberry Bush") on the CD-ROM. Point to the words on the screen as you listen. Encourage students to chime in as they feel comfortable.

Repeat Performances

Use these ideas when you revisit the song:

- Listen and Recite
  Encourage students to work alone or with a partner to chime in on *One Sunny Day* as it is played on the CD-ROM.

- Innovations
  Select students to sing the verse, replacing the action. *This is the way I played in the sand. This is the way I dug in the sand,* etc. Have more able students copy the verse form, filling in a new activity, and then illustrating their verses.

  This is the way we _____,
  _____, _____.
  This is the way we _____,
  *   one sunny day.*

- Send It Home
  Reproduce page 45 for students to take home and share with their families.

One Sunny Day

This is the way we walked to the park,
walked to the park, walked to the park.
This is the way we walked to the park,
one sunny day.

This is the way we flew a kite,
flew a kite, flew a kite.
This is the way we flew a kite,
one sunny day.

This is the way we fed the ducks,
fed the ducks, fed the ducks.
This is the way we fed the ducks,
one sunny day.

This is the way we ate our lunch,
ate our lunch, ate our lunch.
This is the way we ate our lunch,
one sunny day.

At the Park
Storybook

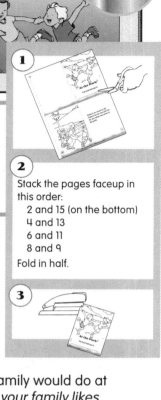

Materials

- *At the Park* reproducible Storybook (pages 47–50), copied back to back for each student, or E-storybook, displayed on a digital projector

Set the Stage

Tell students: *This is a story about a father and two children spending the day at the park.* You may wish to invite students to speculate about what the family might do at the park: *What could the father and the children do for fun at the park?*, etc. Then say: *Let's look at this story together. Let's see how the family has fun at the park.*

Read the Storybook

- Invite students to follow along in their Storybooks as you read the story, pausing to cue students for page turns. (If you are using a digital projector, read the text aloud rather than turning on the audio.)

- Read the story again, one page at a time. Pause to interact with students, using appropriate questioning strategies to elicit language: *Who is this? Where are the children? What is the father doing?*, etc. Use restatement, gestures, or picture clues to help students understand any unfamiliar vocabulary: *Fly means to move through the air. Wind makes the kite fly.*

- After completing the second reading, encourage students to compare what their family would do at the park to those in the story: *Does your family go to the park? Tell me about what your family likes to do together*, etc.

- Go through the story again page by page. Invite volunteers to take turns reading or paraphrasing the text on each page or describing the picture.

Reread the Storybook

- Encourage individuals, partners, or small groups to play the E-storybook on the computer. For their first rereading sessions, be sure students click on the audio icon so they can listen as the text is read aloud. For later rereading, students may wish to leave the audio off and read the text aloud as it is highlighted on the screen.

- An adult, cross-grade tutor, or peer with strong reading skills can lead learners in an "echo" reading of the Storybook, where the leader models reading the text on each page for others to echo.

- Pair a student with less proficient English skills with a more fluent student to reread the Storybook. The more proficient partner can model language or use simple prompts to encourage his or her partner to read or talk about the story.

Follow-Up

- After students are familiar with the story, they may complete the activities on pages 51 and 52.

- Provide copies of the reproducible Storybook for students to take home and share with their families.

At the Park

This book belongs to

_____

There is so much to do!
There's fun for me and fun for you
when we come to the park.

14

3

We've had so much fun,
but the day is almost done.
Now we must leave the park.

2

15

We can look up at the sky
and watch the clouds go by
when we come to the park.

4

13

We can climb up to the top
then slide until we stop
when we come to the park.

11

We can ride around and around
on the merry-go-round
when we come to the park.

9

We can fly our kites up high,
up where the birds can fly
when we come to the park.

12

5

We can dig in the sand
or run hand in hand
when we come to the park.

10

7

Name _____

Fun at the Park

Number the pictures in order.

Draw what you like to do at the park.

Talk About It

Note: Review what each person in the Storybook did at the park. Students make an **X** in the box to show who did what.

Name _____

Who Did It?

Make an **X** to show who did it.

Went to the park			
Sat on the bench			
Flew a kite			
Looked at the clouds			
Went down the slide			
Rode the merry-go-round			

Talk About It

Using the Games

After vocabulary has been introduced through a Poster lesson, students may use the E-games and games with Picture Cards for additional interaction with vocabulary in meaningful contexts.

E-games

The E-games help develop receptive language as students listen to simple directions and commands and then demonstrate comprehension by making choices on the computer. Students have the opportunity to self-correct, following simple directions to "try again" when they respond incorrectly. The motivating, nonthreatening computer environment encourages even reluctant learners to engage in new language. The repetition of language in the E-games also helps students internalize simple language patterns and structures.

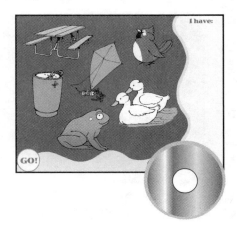

Games with Picture Cards

The games with Picture Cards involve partners or small groups in verbal interaction as they participate in a variety of simple games, ranging from sorting and classifying cards, to charades and Lotto. Because the Picture Cards feature theme-related vocabulary, students will gain additional practice with vocabulary words as they play. They will also negotiate turn-taking, explain their reasoning, make guesses, and use language for other types of purposeful communication. More than anything else, the games with Picture Cards provide a reason to get students talking.

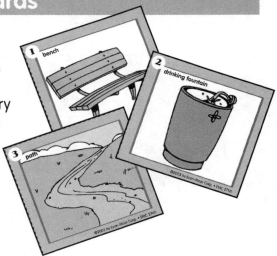

Game 1

E-game 1 provides additional practice with nouns previously introduced.

1 To access Game 1, students go to the main menu and click on Games. This takes them to the game menu.

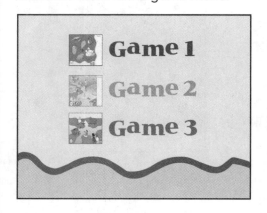

2 Click on Game 1. When the game appears, click on **GO!**.

3 Students listen to the first prompt and click on the item named.

If the correct item is selected, it appears in the answer box.

If the correct item is not selected, students hear *Try again*, and the original direction is repeated so students make a new selection.

4 When all the items in the first set have been found, a second set appears and play continues. When students have successfully responded to all the prompts, they hear applause.

5 When the game has been completed, students make a choice:

To leave Games–click on

To play the same game again–click on **GO!**

To choose a different game–click on

Game 2

E-game 2 provides additional practice with nouns and verbs previously introduced.

1 To access Game 2, students go to the main menu and click on Games. This takes them to the game menu.

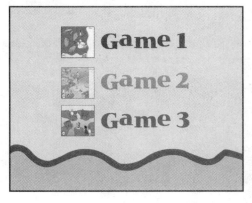

2 Click on Game 2. When the game appears, click on **GO!**.

3 Students listen to the first direction, and then select an answer by scrolling over the action.

If the correct action is scrolled over, the action is performed. Students click on the same action and listen for the next direction.

If the correct action is not selected, students hear *Try again*, and the original direction is repeated so students make a new selection.

4 When the game has been completed, students make a choice:

To leave Games—click on

To play the same game again—click on **GO!**

To choose a different game—click on

Look, Listen, and Speak—At the Park • EMC 2740

Building Fluency

Game 3

E-game 3 provides practice with nouns and verbs previously introduced.

1 To access Game 3, students go to the main menu and click on Games. This takes them to the game menu.

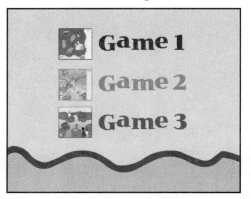

2 Click on Game 3. A map of the park will appear.

When the first close-up of the map appears, click on **GO!**.

3 Students click on the children in the corner, listen to the first direction, and then click on the correct answer.

If the correct answer is selected, students see a red trail that leads them to the next part of the maze.

If the correct answer is not selected, students hear *Try again*, and the original direction is repeated so students make a new selection.

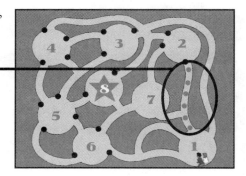

4 When students reach the picnic table, they get a surprise.

5 When the game has been completed, students make a choice:

To leave Games–click on

To play the same game again–click on **GO!**

To choose a different game–click on

Games with Picture Cards

Around the Circle

This game is for a small group directed by a leader (a teacher, aide, volunteer, or cross-grade student).

Materials

- Picture Cards (a selection of any 6 to 12 at a time)

How to Play

1. Students sit in a circle. The leader shows a card and names the item pictured on it. The card is passed to the student on the right, who names the card and passes it to the right until each student has had a turn.

2. Follow a similar procedure to present and name the rest of the cards.

3. Extend the activity by sending the cards around again. This time, the leader models a simple sentence that includes the item on the picture card. After students repeat the sentence, the leader can invite volunteers to model other sentences.

What Do You Have in Your Bag?

This game is for two players.

Materials

- Picture Cards (select 12 to 18 cards to practice)
- two small paper bags
- page 60, reproduced for each player

How to Play

1. Give each player a bag containing the same number of cards.

2. The first student pulls out a card and says, *I have a _____. What do you have?* while showing the card to the other player.

3. The second player pulls out a card and answers, *I have a _____. What do you have?*

4. Play continues back and forth until both players have named all of the cards in their bags.

5. Players write or draw the objects in their bags on their worksheets.

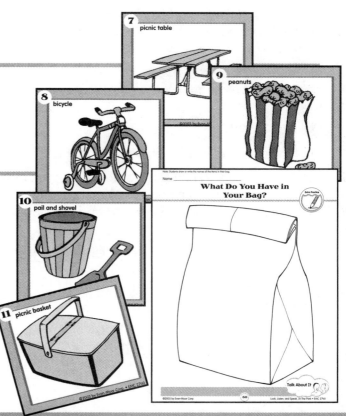

Games with Picture Cards

Memory

This is a game for two. There should be a player and a more language-proficient person to supervise.

Materials

- Picture Cards (choose any picture cards)
- basket for paper bag

How to Play

1. The supervisor lays out the cards faceup (begin with four cards and add more when the player is ready).

2. The supervisor points to each card and says its name. The player echoes the names. Repeat two more times, and then let the player have a minute to study the cards.

3. The player turns his or her back to the cards and names the objects or activities shown on the cards. The supervisor checks to see if the player is correct.

Act It Out

This game is for a small group directed by a leader (a teacher, aide, volunteer, or cross-grade student).

Materials

- Picture Cards 28–44
- basket or paper bag

How to Play

1. Place the cards in the basket or paper bag.

2. The group leader selects a student to pick a picture card from the container. The student pantomimes the activity pictured on the card and asks the group, *What am I doing?*

3. The student who answers correctly gets to perform the next charade.

Encourage students to answer in complete sentences. More advanced students should elaborate whenever possible: *You are throwing a ball. You are digging in the sand. You are drinking water from the fountain.*

Games with Picture Cards

What Goes Together?

This can be played as a card game by three students following the directions below. Or one student may use it for individual practice, sorting the cards and then recording items for each category on the worksheet.

Materials

- Picture Cards (six items each of playground equipment, actions, and animals)
- page 61, reproduced for each player

How to Play

1. Assign a category to each player, giving each one card from his or her category as a starter card.

2. Mix up the Picture Cards and place them facedown in a pile.

3. The first player selects a card and names it. If it is part of his or her category, the card is kept. If not, the card is put on the bottom of the pile.

4. Play progresses in turn. When all cards have been taken (or a specified amount of time has passed), the game is over.

5. Players lay out their six cards so everyone can see them. They then take turns writing the names of items in each category on the worksheet.

Classroom Lotto

Up to four students can play this game. One player calls the picture names as the three other players try to find the pictures on their game boards.

Materials

- picture cards 1–48 to use as calling cards
- game boards on pages 62–64, reproduced and laminated
- small objects or counters for game board markers

How to Play

1. The caller draws a Picture Card from the deck and names the item pictured. (At a more advanced level, the caller names the function of the picture rather than its name.)

2. Players check their game boards to see if they have a picture of the item named, placing a counter on the picture when it is found.

3. The first player to fill a complete row across, down, or diagonally calls out: *Lotto!* To win, the player must correctly name the items (or functions, if playing the advanced version) in the winning row.

4. The winner of the game becomes the caller for the next round.

Note: Students draw or write the names of the items in their bag.

Name _____

What Do You Have in Your Bag?

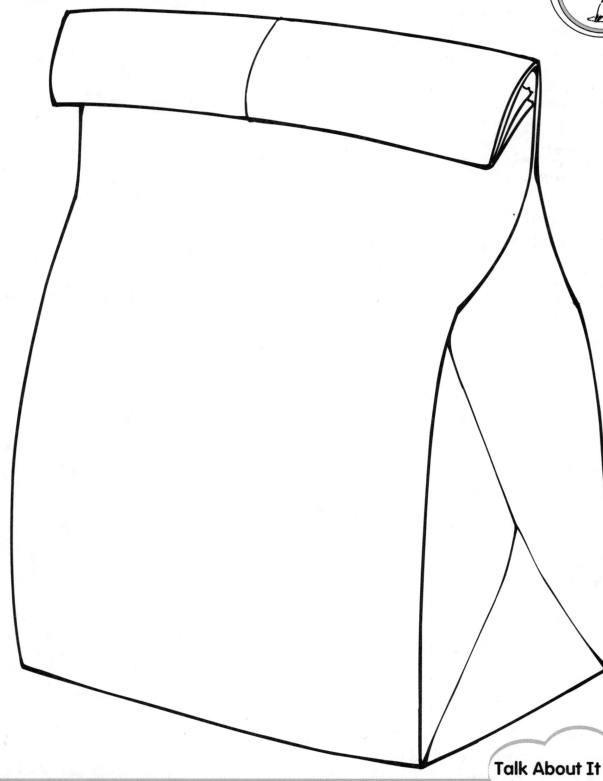

Talk About It

Note: Review the names on the Picture Cards. Explain that the cards should be sorted into sets (Playground Equipment, Animals, Actions). After sorting the cards into three sets, the student writes the names in the correct boxes.

Name _____

What Goes Together?

Sort the cards. Write the names.

Playground Equipment	Animals	Actions

1._____   1._____   1._____

2. _____   2. _____   2. _____

3. _____   3. _____   3. _____

4. _____   4. _____   4. _____

5. _____   5. _____   5. _____

6. _____   6. _____   6. _____

Talk About It

At the Park Lotto

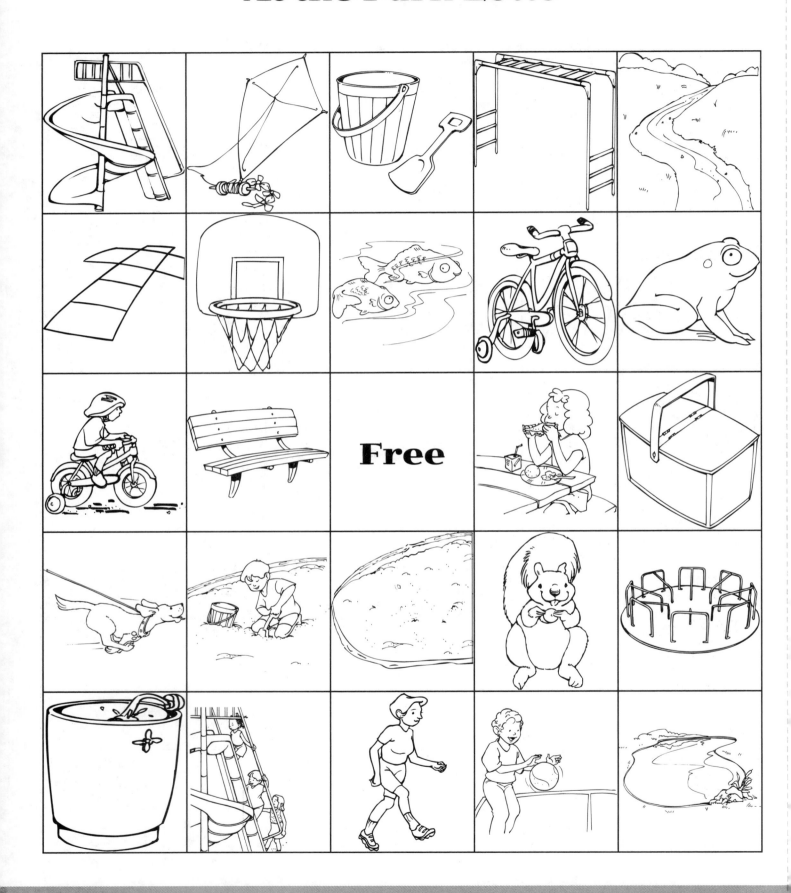

Free

Look, Listen, and Speak—At the Park • EMC 2740

At the Park Lotto

Look, Listen, and Speak—At the Park • EMC 2740

At the Park Lotto

Look, Listen, and Speak—At the Park • EMC 2740

1 bench

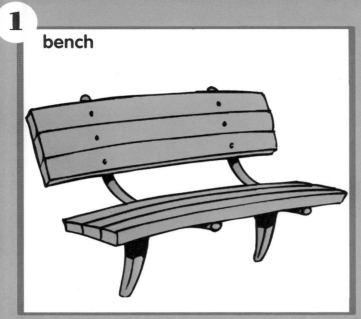

2 drinking fountain

3 path

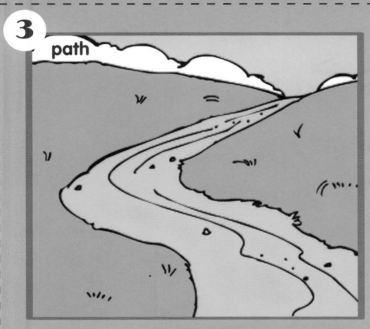

4 pond

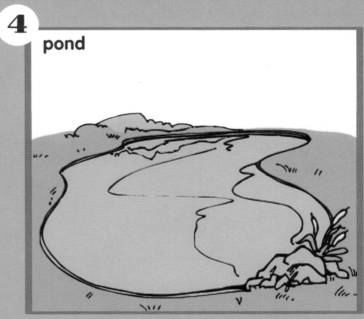

5 kite

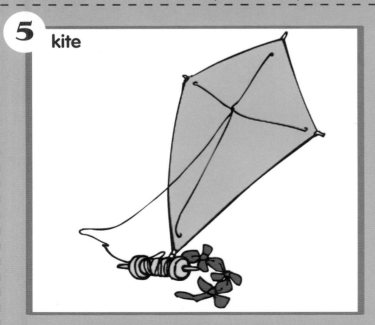

6 sand

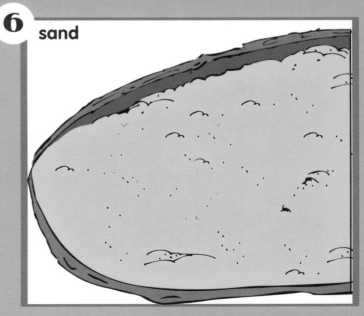

7 picnic table

8 bicycle

9 peanuts

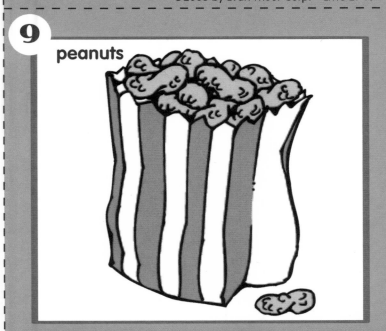

10 pail and shovel

11 picnic basket

12 slide

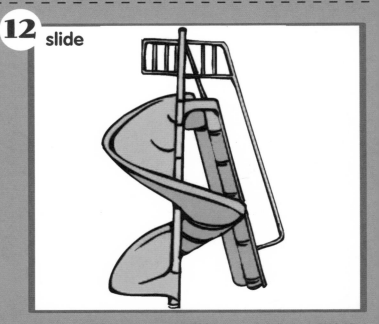

13 merry-go-round

14 monkey bars

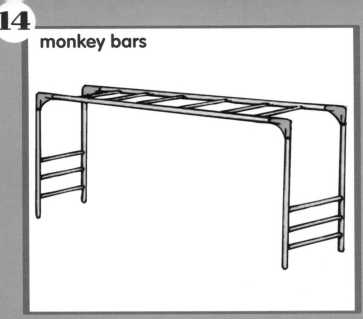

15 jungle gym

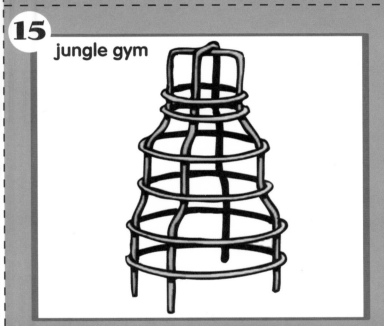

16 basketball hoop

17 hopscotch

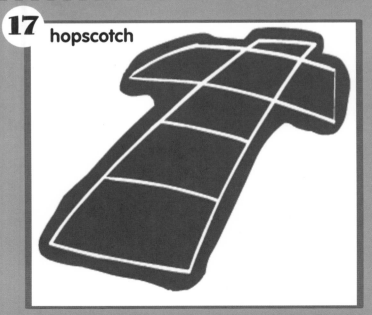

18 foursquare

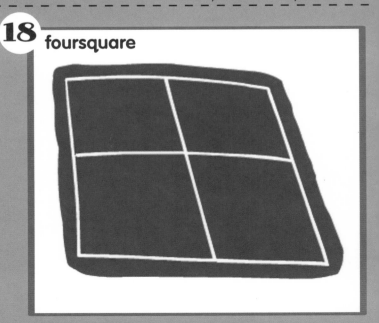

19 baseball field

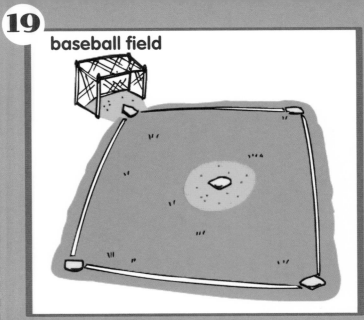

20 dog

21 bird

22 squirrel

23 ducks

24 fish

25 frog

26 grass

27 tree

28 running

29 walking
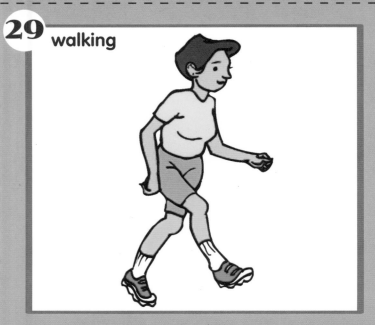

30 riding

31 throwing

32 catching

33 drinking

34 eating

35 flying a kite

36 feeding the squirrels

37 sitting

38 digging

39 pushing

40 climbing

41 swinging

42 bouncing

43 hopping

44 waiting in line

45 he

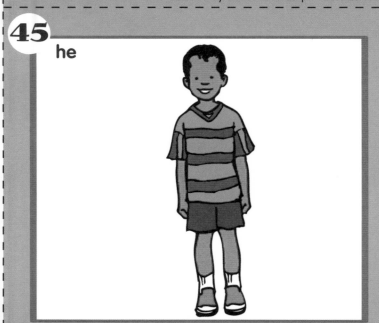

46 she

47 they

48 it